THE HOLY R

The devotion of the Holy Ros
the Church for hundreds of ye   .y Rosary is a
devotion to Our Blessed Mother Mary which includes
the mysteries, or events from the lives of Jesus and
Mary. Learn about the Rosary with fun and
meaningful activities!

Written and Illustrated by Deborah C. Johnson
ISBN 978-1-61796-214-1
Artwork and Text © 2017 Aquinas Kids, Phoenix, Arizona
Printed in China

The first prayer on the Rosary is the Sign of the Cross, on the cross itself.

Color the cross first. Color the beads second.

TALK ABOUT IT...

Rosary means a 'crown of roses', a spiritual bouquet given to the Blessed Mother.

Do you have a rosary?

What is your favorite prayer?

The Apostles' Creed is a prayer that states the basic beliefs of the Catholic Church. It is also prayed on the cross.

Color the words and create a decorative border.

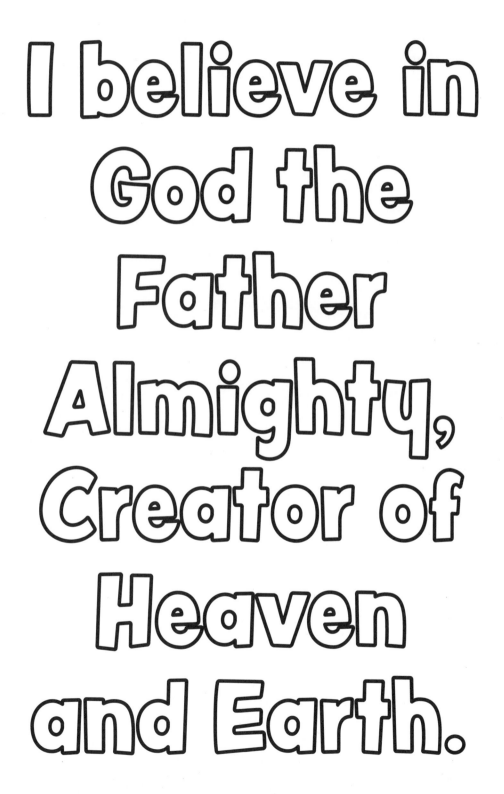

I believe in God the Father Almighty, Creator of Heaven and Earth.

On the first bead, we pray the Our Father.

Draw a picture of what you think heaven looks like.

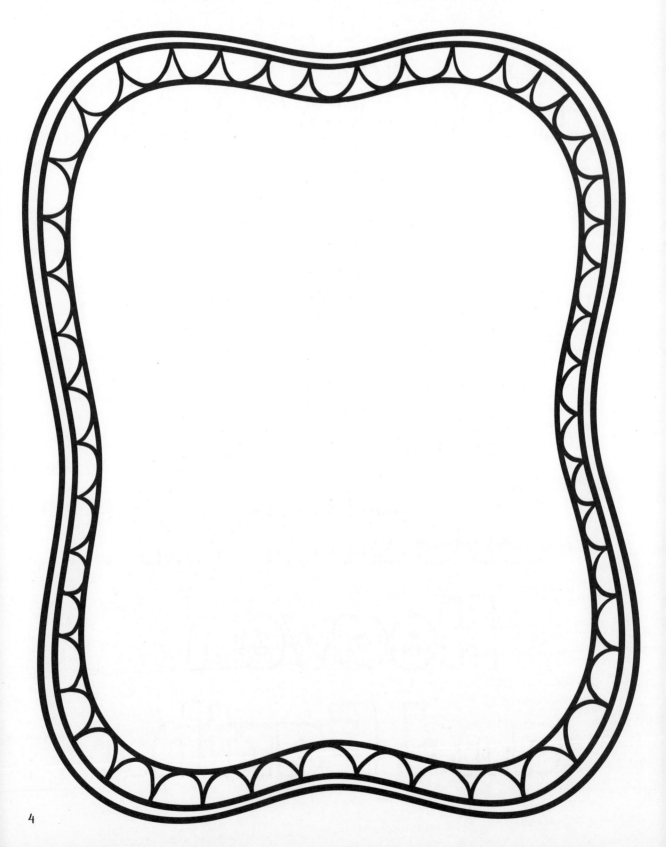

On the next three beads we pray the Hail Mary. Each set of ten beads is called a "decade."

```
G M R M D Q K V R M J Z
A J N O T Y T G E T J N
B J J J S O Y Y T V M Q
R P W R N A R B N V O T
I M Y R K A R A G B J L
E Y A J M P O Y N E B N
L E R L Q B N K S G W X
F R I O E D J U J B E D
L A V Y L O S V T R M L
H L B J V G B L D L V Y
```

_____

Find and circle the words in the list.

Connect the dots around the puzzle. Think about what the Rosary means to you.

HAIL MARY	**GOD**
ANGEL	**ROSARY**
JESUS	**FEAR NOT**
GLORY	**LOVE**
GABRIEL	**OBEY**

At the end of each decade, we pray the Glory Be. It honors God the Father, God the Son, and God the Holy Spirit.

Practice following the hand motions of "the cross" and saying the Glory Be
Color the picture..

1
1. In the name of the Father

2
2. And of the Son

3
3. And of the Holy

4
4. Spirit. Amen.

Our Lady of Fatima visited three young children in Fatima, Portugal, in 1917. She asked them to pray for world peace.

Color the picture of the earth. Add stars, the sun and moon in the background.

TALK ABOUT IT...

What does the word "peace" mean to you?

There are four sets of five "MYSTERIES" or events in the lives of Jesus and Mary. We think about these events and remember them while praying the Rosary.

THE JOYFUL MYSTERIES,
for the early life of Jesus and His Mother, are first.

Decorate and color the word "JOYFUL." Use the extra space to write or draw things that are joyful!

1. THE ANNUNCIATION

The Angel Gabriel visits Mary, and announces that God has chosen her to be the Mother of His Son.

Connect the dots around Mary and color the picture.

2. THE VISITATION

Mary shares her good news with her cousin, Elizabeth.

*Circle the items that Mary would have needed on her trip
to see Elizabeth. Color the pictures.*

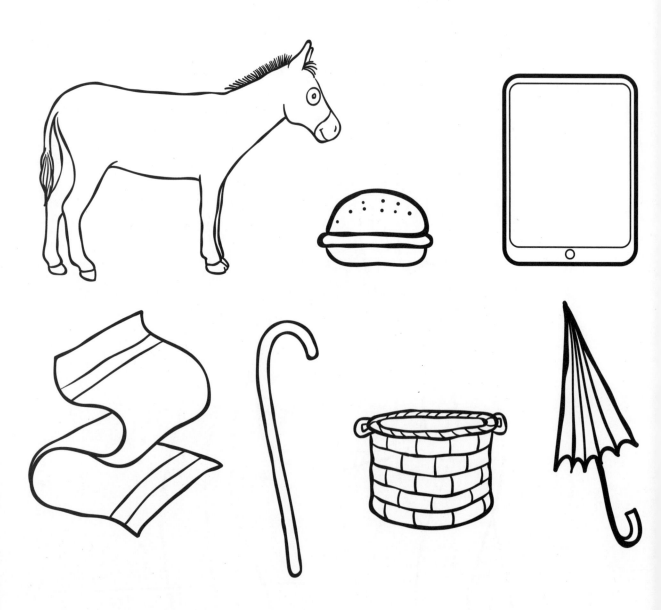

3. THE NATIVITY
Jesus is born in Bethlehem.

Connect the dots around the stable.
Draw Baby Jesus in the manger and add a star above the stable.

TALK ABOUT IT...

What do you think it was like the night Jesus was born?

4. THE PRESENTATION

Mary and Joseph take Baby Jesus to the Temple.

Help Mary and Joseph get to the Temple.

5. THE FINDING OF JESUS IN THE TEMPLE

Joseph and Mary thought Jesus was lost, but they found Him asking questions of the Jewish teachers in the Temple.

How many words can you make from "Holy Temple"? Use the lines to write your words.

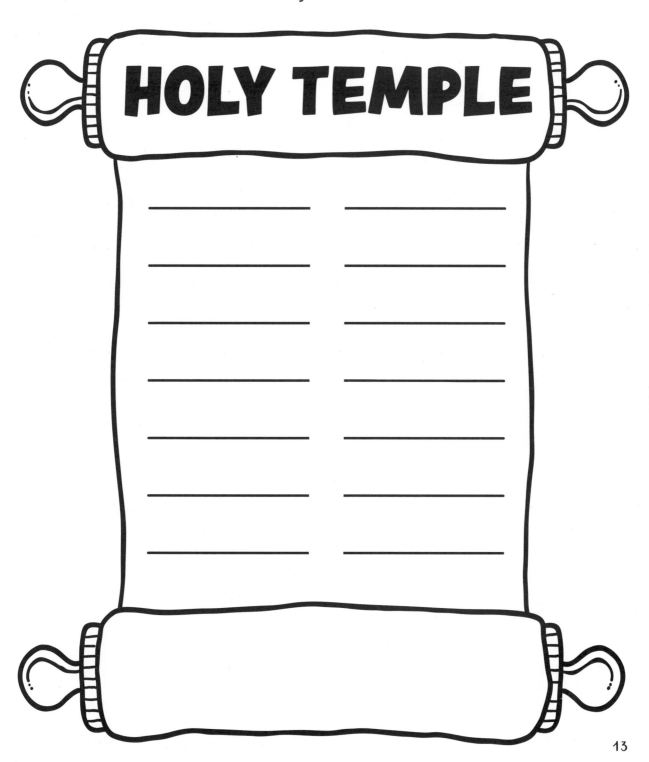

HOLY TEMPLE

THE LUMINOUS MYSTERIES
(THE MYSTERIES OF LIGHT)

These five Mysteries are important events in the life of Jesus as a teacher and healer. Jesus brought a bright light to shine in people's hearts.

Decorate and color the words. Think about what makes you happy.

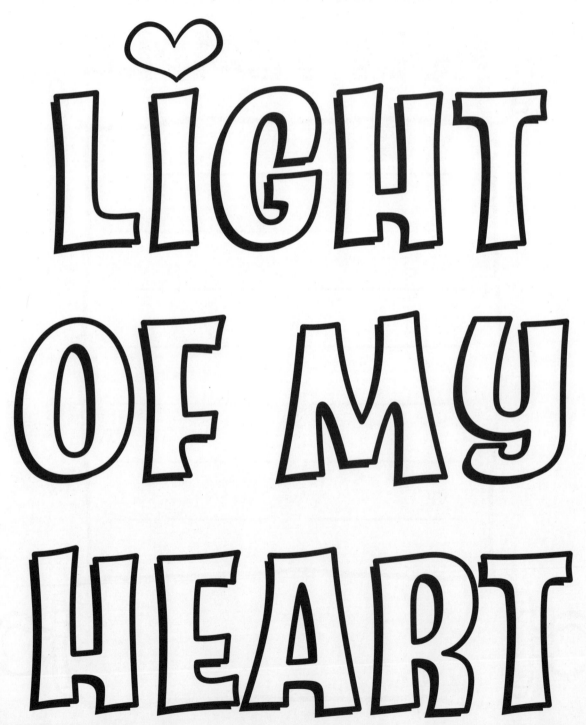

1. THE BAPTISM OF THE LORD
Jesus was baptized by His cousin, John the Baptist.

Connect the dots around the cross and then color. Have you ever been to a Baptism? Describe what you experienced.

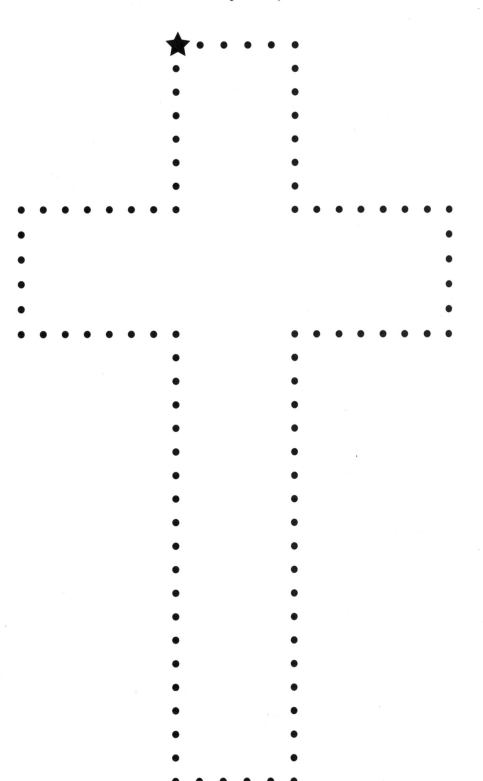

2. THE WEDDING AT CANA
Jesus turned water into wine at a wedding reception.

Circle the objects that belong at a wedding. Color all of the images that do not belong.

3. THE PROCLAMATION OF THE KINGDOM
Jesus tells the people that God's Kingdom is close to them.

Fill the letters with interesting patterns and then color.

4. THE TRANSFIGURATION OF THE LORD

Jesus' face shone like the sun and His clothes became white as the light as He appeared to His Apostles in glory.

GREAT MEN IN THE GOSPELS

```
R E G N U O Y E H T S E M A J
R E D L E E H T S E M A J L R
N T H O M A S N X M E W W R K
X H Q W R P O N T L K J L X D
Y N O E P M T J P N U T B J L
N R T J I M T L A I L R U G B
N E W S L L R T J J L D T X J
P L M A T T H E W U A I L M Z
L Z R R A A Q K Y S D R H N L
L L D X N K W D L M D E Z P Z
Y K Z A D P M M V Q L Z P L R
Z R E Y R L B L K G L V L J N
Y L P J E J Y Y Y R D V L Q V
V X L B W B D Y B D K L T Q X
```

ANDREW	**MATTHEW**
NATHANAEL	**PETER**
JAMES THE ELDER	**PHILIP**
JAMES THE YOUNGER	**SIMON**
JOHN	**THOMAS**
JUDE	**LUKE**

5. THE INSTITUTION OF THE EUCHARIST
At the Last Supper, Jesus changed the bread and wine into His Body and Blood for us.

Decorate the chalice and color the picture. What do the wine and bread represent?

THE SORROWFUL MYSTERIES

When we pray these Mysteries, we remember that Jesus was willing to suffer and die for our sins.

Color the word "Sorrow" in purple. What does sacrifice mean? Draw or write ways that you might sacrifice for others.

1. THE AGONY IN THE GARDEN

The night before Jesus died, He prayed that He would do what God wanted Him to do. It was a difficult and long night for Jesus.

Draw a tree in the background and color a night sky.

2. THE SCOURGING AT THE PILLAR

Pontius Pilate ordered that Jesus be tied to a post and beaten with long whips. He had done nothing wrong.

Color the picture.

Let me never hurt Jesus by any evil word or deed. Keep my body pure and my soul holy.

TALK ABOUT IT...

Jesus loves us very much and wants us to live a healthy lifestyle. What are some things you can do to keep healthy?

3. THE CROWNING WITH THE THORNS

Jesus was dressed in a red cape and a crown of thorns was placed on his head. They made fun of Jesus and the thorns hurt.

Add thorns to the crown and color. Two have been done for you.

4. THE CARRYING OF THE CROSS
Jesus carried His own heavy cross.

Color the picture. In the extra space, write or draw all of the ways you know that Jesus loves you!

THE CRUCIFIXION

```
Z  S  Q  T  R  Z  S  M  Q  R
S  D  O  T  B  P  S  D  T  T
U  N  B  L  E  L  M  A  R  Y
S  A  D  A  I  S  Q  Y  Z  L
E  H  R  A  F  D  S  T  N  Z
J  W  N  D  E  J  E  O  X  D
L  P  A  D  E  M  D  R  R  B
T  S  L  X  T  R  V  X  S  C
```

Find and circle the words in the list.

Draw the cross in the space below:

CROSS	**NAILS**
JESUS	**HANDS**
MARY	**FEET**
SOLDIERS	**SAD**
SPEAR	

THE GLORIOUS MYSTERIES
We celebrate that Jesus is alive and Mary is in Heaven with Him.

Decorate and color the word "Glorious". Fill the background with bright colors.

TALK ABOUT IT...
Celebrate God's love for you this week by sharing this Good News with others!

1. THE RESURRECTION OF JESUS
Many thought Jesus was dead, but He is alive!

Color a beautiful sky behind Jesus.

TALK ABOUT IT...

Describe what it feels like to know that Jesus is alive and watches over us.

2. THE ASCENSION OF JESUS INTO HEAVEN
Jesus tells His Apostles that He must return to Heaven.

Follow the maze from start to finish. Color the background like a map.

START here to spread
the good news that
Jesus lives!

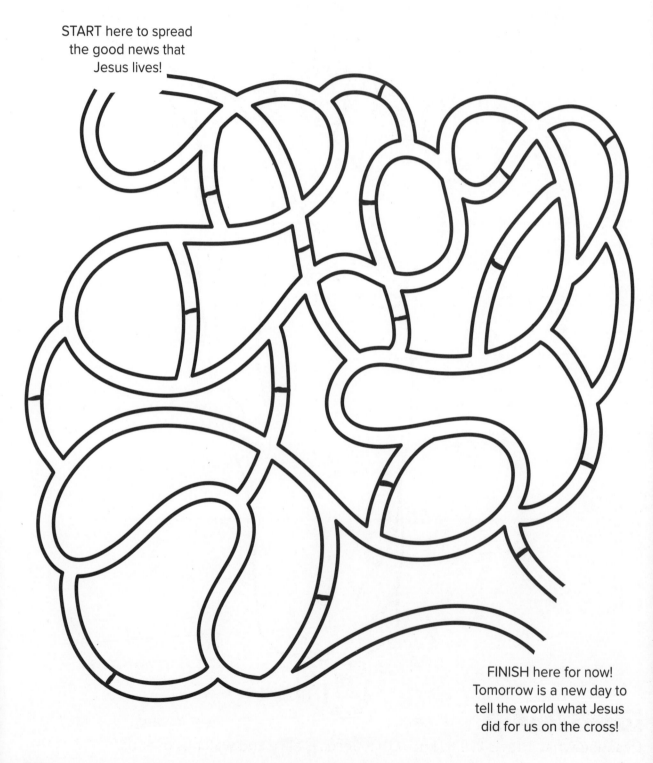

FINISH here for now!
Tomorrow is a new day to
tell the world what Jesus
did for us on the cross!

3. THE DESCENT OF THE HOLY SPIRIT
The Holy Spirit came to help the Apostles.

How many words can you make from "Holy Spirit"?

HOLY SPIRIT

_____   _____

_____   _____

_____   _____

_____   _____

_____   _____

_____   _____

4. THE ASSUMPTION OF THE BLESSED MOTHER

Jesus loved His Mother so much that He took her body to Heaven after she died.

Color the words. In the space below, draw and color six roses.

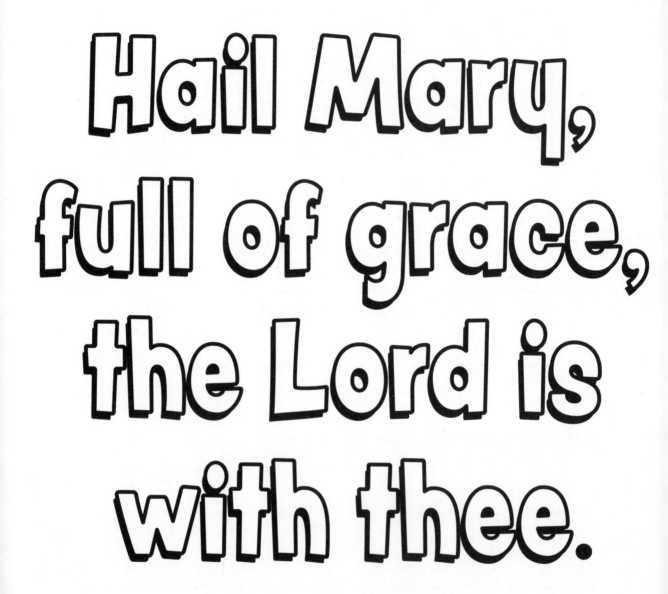

Hail Mary, full of grace, the Lord is with thee.

5. THE CORONATION OF MARY

The Rosary is a circle, like a crown. Honor Jesus and Mary by praying it often. God bless you!.

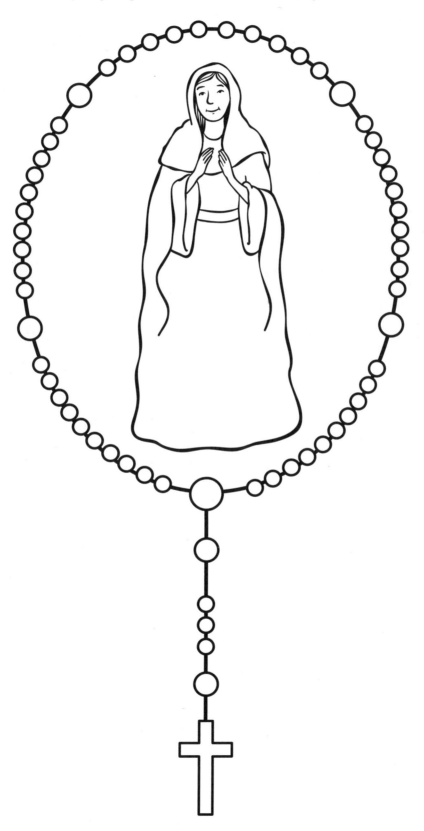

The Holy Rosary honors Mary as the Mother of Jesus